ESSENTIAL CONCEPTS

The Correct Way to Develop Your Rock Voice

by Coreen Sheehan

ISBN 978-0-634-02976-9

7777 W. BLUEMOUND RD. P.O. BOX 13819 MILWAUKEE, WI 53213

In Australia Contact:
Hal Leonard Australia Pty. Ltd.
4 Lentara Court
Cheltenham, Victoria, 3192 Australia
Email: ausadmin@halleonard.com.au

Visit Hal Leonard Online at
www.halleonard.com

Contents

Introduction

Rock technique is probably one of the most misunderstood vocal techniques of all. If you've studied before, I'm sure you've heard voice teachers state that there is "no correct way to sing rock music." I've heard several times from a few of my past instructors, "Screaming or shouting is all you have to know when singing rock." Frustrated and determined, I began to study what it takes to not only have control, but also to maintain a career in singing rock. I've concluded that several aspects come into play: power, dynamics, range, consistency, confidence, and stamina (to get through show after show without damaging your voice).

Rock can be divided into several sub-genres: folk, country, pop, hard rock, and metal. There are certain techniques required to sing within the spectrum of these styles: *head voice* (falsetto), *chest voice* (power), *mixed voice*, *clean tone*, *vibrato*, *vocal whisper*, *growls and grit*, *screams*, and *volume swells.* These are the techniques we will study and scrutinize in this book.

Chapter One
HOW TO STUDY AND IMPROVE YOUR VOICE

Those with no vocal training have probably taught you to warm up by singing songs. While it's true that any warm up for the voice is good, singing songs is *not* the best way to go about it. Why? About 90 percent of rock consists of singing in the middle register, with only a certain amount of notes reaching either higher or lower. Usually you're singing the same notes over and over again—especially when you only sing along with one artist. Also, if your songs are sung in the same range over and over again, the vocal cords will begin to recognize only those notes. Here's why: Vocal cords stretch into a new adjustment with each note sung. When singing scales, you're vocalizing one note at a time and building the muscle memory needed for correct production, stretching by muscle and cartilage movements. Think about it. Anything you do physically is controlled by muscle memory; your voice works in the same way.

Those of you who practice scales without focus or understanding are probably noticing slow progress. You've probably asked yourself, "What is this scale for?" I've been there too, practicing scales in hopes of gaining range, power, and control, but going through the motions of repetitive practice without true focus on what I needed physically (vowel placements, resonance, etc.). I want you to always understand why you're practicing a scale and what it is for. This way you will keep a consistent vocal practice, and you'll notice improvements not only by hearing it, but also feeling the physical movements.

For those of you who already practice scales and understand what to focus on...cool! Hopefully you will learn some new information along the way. It's always a great idea to explore and consume as much information as possible. Filter in new and interesting tidbits to see if it brings you a little closer to your goals. The great thing about music is that it's always evolving and changing. I don't believe you will ever reach a point where you know everything. I also believe you never reach a point where you can truly say, "I'm great. I don't need to learn anymore." If you truly love music, you will always want to learn and improve as much as you can. This way you're always either in the game, or at least hip to it.

Staying Healthy

A singer's health plays an important role. Your vocal cords and the mechanisms surrounding them are affected by the condition of your body.

Fatigue

If you're tired, your voice is usually the first to go. It may get deeper in tone or lower than your normal speaking pitch. If you need to sing in your upper register because your songs call for it, you may need a little extra warm up.

Sickness

If you're sick, you may have a sore throat or swollen lymph nodes. This gives your throat a very uncomfortable, tight feeling, creating an unrelaxed condition to sing in. Head colds or congestion sometimes leave your ears clogged, making it difficult to hear correct pitches at a consistent volume. This can also lead you to overcompensate and incorrectly engage the vocal cords.

Stress

Stress or nervousness can result in muscle tension that can hinder the vocal cords from natural production. Why? Muscles surround the larynx, and when they tighten, a chain reaction of muscle tension sets off, squeezing and constricting the larynx. When this happens, it becomes difficult for the vocal cords to stretch naturally and, of course, stay relaxed.

Health Tricks

Steam

Steam is great for singers with a sore throat, as well as nasal or head congestion. Breathing in warm steam helps soothe swollen membranes and loosen sinus congestion. A steam machine works great because you can place your nose and mouth into the mask, whereby a flow of steam is directed towards the face. If you don't have a steam machine, try this trick. Pour hot water into a bowl, place a towel over your head, and then breathe in and out.

Water

Drinking lots of room temperature water helps moisten the throat. Also, water helps to clear out any phlegm that might be hanging around in the throat. Phlegm inside the larynx can add extra weight to the vocal cords, making it difficult to get natural vibration from them. Why room temperature water? Imagine playing guitar: After you warm up for 20 minutes, you place your fingers on a block of ice for a couple of seconds, and then go back to practicing. Your fingers are going to be a little stiff. That's what happens to your voice when you have cold drinks while singing. It is important to always keep the throat area warm. It's called "warming up" for a reason!

Rest

The voice can be very delicate and sensitive. Think about how you feel when you're tired. What is the first thing your body does? Your voice begins to get deeper and rough sounding. How about when you wake up? What's the last part of you're body to wake up? It's your voice! Getting plenty of rest (a good night's sleep) is important for maintaining a healthy voice. Of course, this can be difficult if your touring schedule is jam-packed and all over the map. If you can't sleep, close your eyes and try to relax on your downtime.

Nutrition

Okay, how many times have we heard, "You are what you eat"? I know we musicians are sometimes scrapping together money to eat. But if you're eating pizza, cheeseburgers, smoothies, or even cereal with milk, you're more than likely going to have *phlegm*. This is due to the dairy products and fatty foods. *Phlegm* likes to hang on the vocal cords and makes you feel the need to clear your throat. A lot of singers avoid dairy products before singing. Fatty foods can weigh you down as well, leaving you feeling full and tired.

When going to a vocal lesson, session, rehearsal, or show, be aware of what you're eating and drinking beforehand. If you like dairy products and are prone to a lot of phlegm, drink a lot of water and do a good warm up before singing. When you sing and the vocal cords vibrate, the phlegm will shake off and kick back up into the throat. Try not to keep clearing your throat, though—drink and sing through it. Clearing the throat over and over abuses the vocal cords—they slam together and swell, leaving you a little sore—so try to avoid it.

Acid Reflux

If you're prone to acid reflux, avoid eating right before you start to sing. Singing after eating can kick up stomach acid, which produces phlegm. If you have a severe case of acid reflux, it can climb up the esophagus and into the larynx, which, in turn, can burn and swell the vocal cords. In many cases, this happens during sleep, so try not to eat too close to bedtime; it's easier for stomach acid to travel up the esophagus when lying down.

Sore Throat

If your throat is sore, try peppermint tea or throatcoat tea with some honey. Both of these are available at your local grocery store, health food store, or pharmacy.

Things to Avoid

Dairy Products

Dairy products, like milk, cheese, and mayonnaise, produce extra phlegm adding weight to the vocal cords. This creates difficulty in achieving a correct stretch of the vocal cords right away, inhibiting free vibrations.

Smoking

Everyone asks, "Does smoking really affect my voice?" The answer is yes! Physically, the heat from tobacco smoke burns the vocal cords, causing them to become irritated and swollen. I smoked for years, and I've always had a great, low-register voice. I could sing in my upper register, but warming up was a more difficult and longer process. Producing a thin, light tone (i.e., singing a high-register ballad) was a struggle at times. When I quit smoking, my body went through a cleansing process, so I had a lot of phlegm coming up. (I know that sounds disgusting.) I went through strange problems with register changes and vocal control, too. After about four months of inconsistencies, I got a hold of my voice. I realized how easy and free my voice felt in my upper register; it felt effortless to sing, and I could sing for longer durations.

Practicing with the CD vs. Keyboard

Practicing with the CD will definitely help for two reasons: (1) You will be listening to the guide vocal examples, and (2) you may have no prior keyboard experience. However, if you can accompany yourself it would be much more beneficial, because it's easier to troubleshoot when you can see the notes in front of you—especially when your voice is challenged from sickness, fatigue, or allergies.

Understanding Keyboard Notes

In the scale exercises, I will refer to the notes on a keyboard by numbers. It is important to understand what registers you are practicing, because when you know your vocal range you will be able to address the areas of your voice that need more training.

An *octave* is a sequence of 8 notes. On the keyboard, middle C will be known as zero. The octave below middle C will be referred to as a minus. For example, the first B note below middle C is B-1. The notes that follow will be B♭-1, A-1, A♭-1, etc. So, the octave below B♭-1 is B♭-2. The octave below B♭-2 is B♭-3, and so on.

Going up, this system works the exact same way, but with pluses. The first note above middle C will be known as C♯+1. The notes that follow are D+1, D♯+1, E+1, and so on. The octave up from the C♯+1 is C♯+2. The octave up from C♯+3 will be know as C♯+4, etc.

Chapter Two
2 HOW THE VOICE MECHANISM WORKS

Some singers think they only have one register to sing in, so that's the only one they practice. This creates an imbalance within the vocal cords. For example, if the low register is easier to sing in, it gets stronger while the upper register remains weak. Both registers need to be isolated, worked on, and practiced to be built up evenly. While one effort is stretching the vocal cords, the other end is holding.

There can be pitch problems if one side is stronger than the other. Say you went to the gym and only worked out the right side of your body, just because you're right handed. What would happen? Well, after a while, your right side would be stronger than your left. The same scenario can happen with your vocal cords if your practice is one-sided. So, when singing in the upper and lower registers, the vocal cords must have the correct stretching and positioning to produce pitch.

The Cricothyroid Muscles & Thyroid Cartilage (Lower Register)

The *cricothyroid* muscles pull forward and down, pulling the thyroid cartilage, stretching the front of the vocal cords. From now on I will refer to this as thyroid effort. The vocal cords are now in a stretched position, because the arytenoid cartilage and muscles are holding the back of the vocal cords in position. When air comes up, the vocal cords vibrate and produce sound.

The Cricoarytenoid Muscles & Arytenoid Cartilages (Upper Register)

The *cricoarytenoid* muscles pull back and upward, pulling the arytenoid cartilages, stretching the back of the vocal cords. From now on I will refer to this as arytenoid effort. This stretching is compounded by the thyroid effort holding the front of the vocal cords. When air comes up, the vocal cords vibrate and produce sound.

The Larynx

Inside the larynx lies the vocal cords. This is where the voice is produced! The larynx consists of cartilages and muscles, as shown below:

1. Vocal Cords
2. Thyroid Cartilage
3. Cricothyroid Muscles
4. Arytenoid Cartilage
5. Cricoarytenoid Muscles
6. Cricoid Thyroid Cartilage

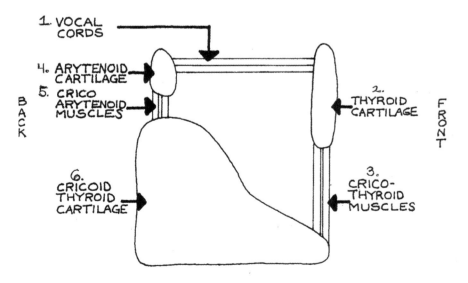

Inside your throat are swallowing muscles surrounding the larynx. Have you noticed that the majority of men have stronger lower registers than women, and vice versa (women have strong upper registers)? This is because the majority of men have developed their speaking voices using the thyroid effort, while women tend to use the arytenoid effort. But everyone has both thyroid and arytenoid mechanisms, making dual-register production possible. Have you ever tried to imitate a high-pitched cartoon character voice like Minnie Mouse? If you can imitate that voice, then you are using the arytenoids. *If you can speak that pitch, you can sing that pitch!* The key is learning how to use both mechanisms naturally and correctly. Understanding how the voice works provides answers to why some vocalizing may seem difficult in a few areas, but easier in others.

To constantly practice singing might show some improvement, but if you are singing incorrectly, you are only reinforcing bad habits. Singing with knowledge helps you achieve a positive vocal practice. You will sharpen your listening skills, become in touch with what sensations are correct, and become more aware of the sensations that can cause damage if used constantly. Overall, you can gain more confidence by knowing correct vocal production.

For example, if your car breaks down and you know nothing about cars, you are not going to be able to fix even the simplest problem. If you study a basic auto class, you'll most likely be able to diagnose the problem. If it's nothing major, you will probably be able to fix it.

Breathing

Most vocalists know that the *diaphragm* is where we breathe from, but it's also our support system while singing. The diaphragm is a large muscle that sits below the lungs. When we inhale, the diaphragm expands (this is physically visible), and when we exhale, the diaphragm contracts and lifts. Some singers focus too much on diaphragmatic breathing, and, in some cases, push so hard that the vocal cords can't withstand the air pressure. The vocal cords must separate to allow the forced air to come through. (Common names for this bad habit are "pushing" and "overblowing.") The action of breathing should happen with ease and freedom—not with great physical force or effort. Of course the breath is very important for singing, because, without breathing, the vocal cords can't vibrate.

Breathing while singing should be as natural as speaking. If I want to do a simple thing, like say "Hello," I wouldn't think:

1   Take a breath.
2   Say "Hello."
3   Take another breath.

Get the point? You naturally take in air without thinking about it. Why? Because it's natural; it's what's called an involuntary reflex. The only time singers need to focus on breathing is when singing with obstacles:

Filling Up with Too Much Air

Some singers do this for fear of not having enough air to get through a long phrase. When you take in too much air and expel it, the air pressure underneath the vocal cords is far too great, and can be so much that the cords separate, allowing too much air to escape.

Holding Your Breath

Singers often do this in preparation for singing the first note of a phrase: For example, in the beginning of a verse, chorus or scales. Holding your breath, even for a second, causes the muscles to tense, starting a chain reaction of muscle tension—the last thing any vocalist wants. Also, the force of the air pressure, when released, may be too great. This, once again, can cause the vocal cords to separate,

Not Replenishing the Breath

When you take breaths over and over and never exhale before each new breath, it can feel as if you have no air, when your lungs really have too much. Why? If you're not exhaling the unused breath at the end of a phrase, taking in more air is basically hyperventilating yourself.

Breathing Through Your Nose

Breathing through your nose closes the nasal passages, so you should always breathe through your mouth. Also you'll never be able to get a quick enough breath if you breathe through your nose. When you're singing fast-tempo songs or quick, run-on lyrics, you must be able to take a quick breath. Also, breathing through your mouth opens the throat area, creating a relaxed condition.

Singing Too Late or Too Early

When you breathe through your mouth, you should feel the air hit the back of your throat (*Oropharynx*). We call that the *cold spot*, because the air feels cool. As soon as you feel it, come right back into singing.

The Three Pharynxes and Vowel Placement

The *pharynx* is a long tube that spans from behind the larynx to the lower-back part of the head. It has three sections: *Laryngopharynx, oropharynx,* and *nasopharynx*. These sections are responsible for our resonance when singing. We will shortly begin to understand how important this resonance is, but for now, let's go over the three different pharynxes sections and learn what takes place in each.

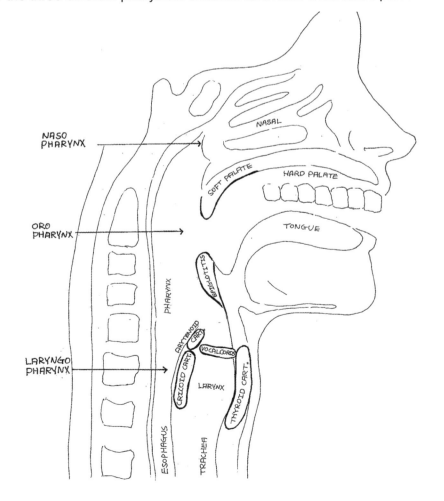

Laryngopharynx

The *laryngopharynx* houses the *larynx*, *epiglottis*, and *pharynx*.

- The *larynx* (also known as the "Voice Box") is where production starts with the voice. The outer shell of the larynx protects the vocal cords, thyroid and arytenoid muscles (and the thyroid, arytenoid cartilages and the cricoid thyroid cartilage.)

- The *epiglottis* is a flexible cartilage attached to the rear base of the tongue. The epiglottis acts as a door to the larynx. When the epiglottis stands erect (straight up), it allows an opening during respiration and vocalization. When the epiglottis moves back and down, it closes the larynx opening, making it ready for swallowing food or liquids.

* The *pharynx* resembles a tube that runs from behind the larynx up to the head. It also plays an important role in resonance.

Oropharynx

The *oropharynx* is located behind the mouth where the uvula, soft and hard palates, tongue, mouth and lips are.

- The *uvula* is attached to the soft palate. When relaxed, it faces down, leaving space in the passageway for resonance. But when the uvula moves backwards, it shuts the passageway where air is trying to go up into the nasopharynx.

- The *hard palate* is where you send air to, acting as a fulcrum that sends air up to the nasopharynx. I will mention the hard palate quite a bit in our exercises because it plays a major role in resonance.

- The tongue, mouth, and lips are very important because they form the words we speak and sing. The tongue helps with vowel pronunciation, while the mouth helps form the vowels. The shape of the lips attract the resonance focus.

Nasopharynx

The *nasopharynx* is where the *superior turbinate*, *middle turbinate*, and *inferior turbinate* are.

- The turbinates act as resonance chambers, contributing to a mask resonance, but I'll refer to them in a more familiar term: *sinus cavities*. Above the sinus cavities are other spaces contributing to head resonance.

Vowel Placement

When singing, we naturally lean the breath of the vowel into the hard palate (as long as there are no obstructions). No matter what language you sing, you bring out the most open vowel sound, because it's how the voice flows over the melody. Whether you have a very melodic vocal style or are using effects such as a raspy voice, the melody is sung on the most open vowels. It would be impossible to sing on the consonants, because it's a closed production inside the mouth. In every language, we have EE, EH, AH, OH, and OO vowel sounds. In order to feel where the hard palate is located, place the tip of your tongue on the roof of your mouth, behind the front teeth. Glide the tongue backwards and you will notice that most of it is hard (hard palate) and then begins to get soften up (*soft palate*) towards the back of the mouth.

Hard Palate vs. Soft Palate

The difference between the hard and the soft palate vowel placements is in the tone. When singing contemporary styles such as rock, we lean the air into the hard palate for a much brighter, fuller, and forward tone. This makes it much easier for the microphone to pick up and project the voice. Especially when singing rock, we need the voice to be forward and projected as much as possible. When playing with a band, usually all instruments are loud because of the amplification. The voice, unfortunately, does not have a volume control to turn up to 10. We need the voice to remain forward and consistent for the microphone to pick up and project it at a level that is balanced with the amplified instruments.

The soft palate is where we would lean the air of vowels if we wanted to produce a classical vocal tone. (The tone of the voice is further back in the mouth, but still sounds full.) Many singers that have had classical training who attempt singing rock often ask, "How can I change my voice to have a more authentic rock sound?" The answer lies in leaning the air of the vowels into the hard palate!

When air travels up from the diaphragm and hits the vocal cords, they vibrate and produce sound. This sound travels from the laryngopharynx to the oropharynx, into the mouth (where we form vowels), where it is then leaned into the hard palate. The air bounces off the hard palate, travels back up into the oropharynx, and reaches the nasopharynx where we have head resonance.

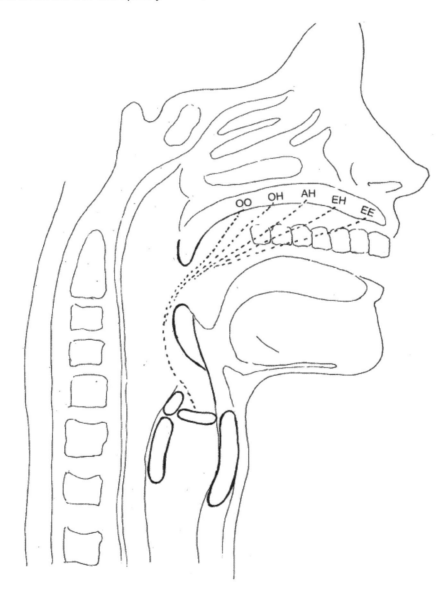

Vowel Formation

The shape of your mouth changes as it forms each vowel sound. When singing vowels, check that you open your mouth by slightly dropping your jaw. Below are examples of mouth formation for each vowel:

Picture 1

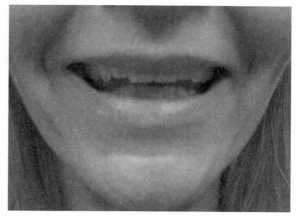

The E Vowel

The jaw will drop a little to allow the mouth to open up, forming the E vowel. The mouth formation should resemble a relaxed smile, allowing your sound to stay bright. Doing this will help keep the E vowel forward in your mouth, which is important when you get into the lower section of your *"Red Voice."*

Picture 2

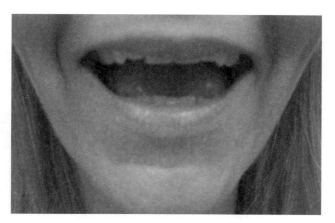

The EH Vowel

To form the EH vowel, drop the jaw slightly more than the E vowel. The mouth formation will be slightly more open than the E vowel.

Picture 3

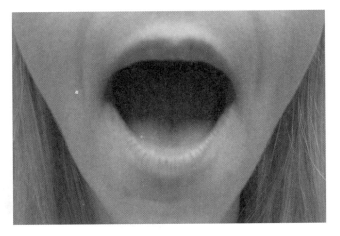

The AH Vowel

The AH vowel can be easy to produce, because it is the most open of all the vowels. The AH is a more natural, open formation, keeping the throat more relaxed and open. The jaw should be dropped more than the EH vowel, making the mouth look fully open.

Picture 4

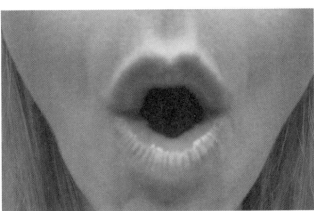

The OH Vowel

To form the OH vowel, drop the jaw, but not as much as with the AH vowel. The lip formation will be important when forming this vowel.

Picture 5

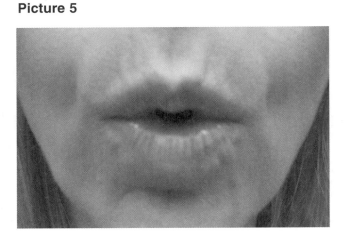

The OO Vowel

To form the OO vowel, drop the jaw slightly less than the OH vowel. Using the lips (slightly puckered, but relaxed) will help form this vowel, especially in the upper register. In the lower register, the OO vowel should have less of a pucker. This will allow the OO vowel sound to open up and resemble the "ewww" sound.

Resonance

Resonance happens when sounded vibration bounces around the empty chambers of the chest, mouth, head, and nasal cavity. For example, if you have ever yelled in a cave or long tunnel, then you've heard your voice echo (resonate) over and over again. The tone of the voice sounds much fuller and richer with resonance than without it. A perfect balance of vocal tone will have equal bass, middle, and treble frequencies. A voice that does not have resonance sounds weaker in volume and not as pleasing to the ear due to its lack of balance.

When singing, it is resonance that gives the voice three important characteristics:
  · Volume and power
  · An evenly balanced tone
  · Sustain

Let's take an acoustic guitar for example. The acoustic guitar doesn't have to be plugged into an amplifier to be heard, so how does it sustain when the strings are struck? How does it have volume and power? Why does it have a solid, balanced tone? All these things are produced by the sound resonating and bouncing inside the body of the guitar.

Resonance Locations

Everyone who feels resonance describes similar sensations. Listed below are some common physical descriptions:

  · **Head:** A buzzing or tingling sensation felt at the top of the head. The sound rings in the ears and head.
  · **Mask:** A vibration in the face around the nose area (where your sinuses are). The volume seems louder in the head, the ears ring, and the sound is more powerful than what you would experience with head resonance.
  · **Chest:** A vibration and a tingling felt in your chest area, as if the voice is coming from a deeper location. Chest resonance is the most powerful tone.

The most commonly used resonances when singing in rock are in the chest and mask. Many powerful songs will demand them simultaneously.

Chapter Three
ENGAGING THE "RED VOICE" (LOWER REGISTER)

3

One of the most difficult facets of vocal training is not being able to see how the voice should be positioned for each note. If you play guitar, it's easy to see where your fingers should be placed and how to play. It's the same with keyboards, drums, bass, etc. But with the voice, the first thing you must do is visualize, then physically feel the movements and sensations while singing. And, of course, developing your ears to distinguish the best sounds is a prerequisite. When singing in the lower registers, the tone of the voice should be rich, thick, and dark. I call this your *"Red Voice."*

When singing these scales, it is important to focus on particular sensations and sounds. At first, you're going to be thinking a lot when singing these scales. Remember, you're exercising your vocal cords and also developing muscle memory. In the long run, this type of concentration won't be as intense when you start performing.

Finger Placement

While exercising in the lower register, place your fingers on each side of your thyroid cartilage. If you don't know where that is, take a finger and find your Adam's Apple. Move slightly downward, placing two fingers on each side of the cartilage. This is your thyroid cartilage–the front section of your larynx. The physical movements can be felt from the thyroid cartilage when singing in the lower register. You will feel a vibration immediately when correctly engaging the thyroid. In addition, when singing notes that descend more than a half step at a time, you will feel the thyroid cartilage move slightly downward. Conversely, when ascending more than a half step, you will feel the thyroid cartilage shift slightly upward.

These movements happen because, with each half step, the vocal cords stretch into a new position. In the first exercise (4-note scales), the starting note to the second note is 2 1/2 steps down, the second to the third is a whole step up, and the third to the fourth note is 2 whole steps down. This exercise requires significant movement of the vocal cords, so the thyroid effort is working to stretch them. When exercising the half-note scales, the vocal cords stretch only slightly for each half note. Because it's such a subtle adjustment, you won't feel significant movements from the thyroid cartilage, but you *will* feel the vibration from the first to the last note of the exercise. This vibration happens when air comes up and strikes the vocal cords. If you let go of the thyroid cartilage while singing the lowest notes of your range, your vocal tone will be airy and breathy. Often, vocalists will associate a breathy voice with lack of diaphragmatic support, but many times it's due to the incorrect stretch of the vocal cords, often because the thyroid effort is weak.

4-Note Scales

These 4-note scales are usually easier for guys to sing, because men normally speak using their thyroid effort. Girls, if you can do the 4-note scales, by all means go for it.

Note: You may not be able to do all of these scales on the first try. That's completely normal! Remember, you are probably exercising areas of your voice that haven't really been used before. Start by singing the easier sections first, then progress to the more challenging areas. Your voice will appreciate your patience.

Listen first to the vocal examples as a reference point, then sing on the repeat.

4-note scales will start at G-1, descend to B-2, and return to the note G-1.

4-note scales

The EH Vowel Using the "Red Voice"

When singing the EH vowel, drop the jaw slightly more than when singing the E vowel. (Refer to picture #2, Vowel Formation.)

1. Place your fingers on the front of your larynx.

2. As soon as you feel the cold spot, start singing the first note.

3. Lean the air of the EH vowel into the hard palate, and focus on keeping it there when moving from note-to-note.

4. Do not sing *staccato* (separated) on each note. Blend the EH vowel into each note. Keep in mind that the EH vowel should not be swelling in and out.

5. Focus on not fading off of your last note, making it as strong as the first 3 notes. If you hear yourself sliding off of the last note, correct yourself. This is a bad habit when executing scales.

6. The EH vowel on the 4th note should be sung as AA, not AE. This means the E sound should not be enunciated on the ending note. Listen to the CD examples as a reference.

PLAY TRACK #1

The E Vowel Using the "Red Voice"

Allow your jaw to relax and slightly drop. You don't want to have tension in your jaw, or else you'll have a tight sounding E vowel. Remember to form a big E sound that feels almost as big as the EH vowel. (Refer to picture #1, Vowel Formation.)

1. Place your fingers on the front of your larynx.

2. As soon as you feel the cold spot, start singing the first note.

3. Place the air of the E vowel as far forward in your hard palate as you can. Try and keep a slight smile on your most difficult notes in the lower section of the "Red Voice."

4. The tongue should remain forward throughout the entire scale.

5. Do not sing staccato. Blend the E vowel into each note, but it should not be swelling in and out.

6. Focus on not fading off of your last note of the scale, making it as strong as the first 3 notes. If you hear yourself sliding off of the last note, correct yourself.

PLAY TRACK #2

The AH Vowel Using the "Red Voice"

When singing the AH vowel, drop the jaw slightly more than when singing the EH vowel. (Refer to picture #3, Vowel Formation.)

1. Place your fingers on the front of your larynx.

2. As soon as you feel the cold spot, start singing your first note.

3. Check and see if you are blending the AH vowel into each note. The breath of the AH vowel should be placed right behind where the EH vowel would be (middle of the hard palate). You should keep this placement throughout the entire scale. A common bad habit is to move its placement back and forth, while descending from the first to the second note, and from the third to the fourth note.

4. Also check to see that your tongue remains forward throughout the entire scale.

5. Do not sing staccato. Blend the AH vowel into each note. The AH vowel should not be swelling in and out.

6. Focus on not fading off of your last note of the scale, making it as strong as the first 3 notes. If you hear yourself sliding off of the last note, correct yourself. This is a bad habit when executing scales.

PLAY TRACK #3

The OH Vowel Using the "Red Voice"

The jaw may be dropped in the same manner as the AH vowel when singing. Your lips will be helping you form the OH vowel. (Refer to picture #4, Vowel Formation.)

1. Place your fingers on the front of your larynx.

2. As soon as you feel the cold spot, start singing your first note.

3. Focus on engaging an OH sound on the first note. If you are having difficulty placing the air of the OH vowel forward in the hard palate, place an "h" sound in front of it. Pulse on the word "ho," quickly shooting the air straight up into the hard palate.

4. Check to see that your tongue remains forward throughout this scale.

5. Do not sing staccato. Blend the OH vowel into each note. The OH vowel should not be swelling in and out.

6. Focus on not fading off of your last note of the scale, making it as strong as the first 3 notes. If you hear yourself sliding off of the last note, correct yourself. This is a bad habit when executing scales.

PLAY TRACK #4

The OO Vowel Using the "Red Voice"

The last vowel in this exercise will be the OO vowel. Your lips will be helping to form this vowel correctly, and your jaw will be dropped slightly. This vowel should be enunciated like the word "ew,"—the sound you make when you're grossed out. That's a big OO vowel sound. (Refer to picture #5, Vowel Formation.)

1. Place your fingers on the front of your larynx.

2. As soon as you feel the cold spot, start singing the first note.

3. The air of the OO vowel will be in the back of the hard palate, even though you may feel the vibrations more on your lips.

4. Check to see that your tongue remains forward throughout the scale.

5. Do not sing staccato. Blend the OO vowel into each note. The OO vowel should not be swelling in and out.

6. Focus on not fading off of your last note of the scale, making it as strong as the first 3 notes. If you hear yourself sliding off of the last note, correct yourself. This is a bad habit when executing scales.

PLAY TRACK #5

4 Half-Step Scales

It's quite common for women to have a difficult time singing in the lower register. Many female singers have been led to believe that they simply don't have it, but I'm here to say that you can improve your voice in this area—you just have to exercise the vocal cords properly by using your thyroid effort. Using these half-note exercises will help you correctly develop the thyroid mechanisms. Singing in half steps allows time for the cords to gradually stretch. "Gradually" is key here, because we are trying to build the muscle memory and develop an area that hasn't been worked before. Try to imagine each note moving forward, straight out of your mouth, instead of going down. When you feel comfortable with this exercise, move on to the 2-note scales.

Listen first to the vocal example as a reference point, then sing on the repeat.

The 4 half-step scales start at B-1, descend to F-1 (but won't return back to the starting note.)

4 half-step scales

The EH Vowel Using the "Red Voice"
When singing the EH vowel, drop the jaw slightly more than when singing the E vowel. (Refer to picture #2, Vowel Formation.)

1. Place your fingers on the front of your larynx.

2. As soon as you feel the cold spot, start singing the first note.

3. When you engage the thyroid effort, maintain the vibration throughout the 4 notes.

4. Lean the air of the EH vowel into the hard palate. It should remain still when moving from note to note.

5. Focus on blending the EH vowel into each note.

6. Try not to let go of the thyroid effort when moving from note to note. Focus on not fading off the last note of the scale.

7. The tongue should remain forward, and your volume should remain consistent throughout the scales.

PLAY TRACK #6

The E Vowel Using the "Red Voice"

Allow your jaw to relax and slightly drop. You don't want to have tension in your jaw or else you'll have a tight sounding E vowel. Remember to form a big E sound that feels almost as big as the EH vowel. (Refer to picture #1, Vowel Formation.)

1. Place your fingers on the front of your larynx.

2. As soon as you feel the cold spot, start singing the first note.

3. When you engage the thyroid, maintain the vibration you're feeling throughout the 4 notes.

4. Place the air of the E vowel as far forward in your hard palate as you can. Try and keep a slight smile on your most difficult notes in the lower section.

5. Focus on blending the E vowel into each note.

6. Try not to let go of the thyroid effort when moving from note to note. Focus on not fading off the last note of the scale.

7. The tongue should remain forward, and your volume should remain consistent throughout the scales.

PLAY TRACK #7

The AH Vowel Using the "Red Voice"

When singing the AH vowel, drop the jaw slightly more than when singing the EH vowel. (Refer to picture #3, Vowel Formation)

1. Place your fingers on the front of your larynx.

2. As soon as you feel the cold spot, start singing the first note.

3. Lean the AH vowel into the middle of the hard palate. Focus on blending the AH vowel into each note. A common bad habit is to move its placement back while descending the scales.

4. The tongue should remain forward, and your volume consistent throughout the scales.

PLAY TRACK #8

The OH Vowel Using the "Red Voice"

The jaw may be dropped in the same manner as the AH vowel when singing. Your lips will help you form this vowel properly. (Refer to picture #4, Vowel Formation.)

1. Place your fingers on the front of your larynx.

2. As soon as you feel the cold spot, start singing the first note.

3. Focus on engaging the OH sound on the first note. If you are having difficulty, place it forward in the hard palate and put an "h" sound in front of the OH vowel. Pulse on the word "ho," quickly shooting the air straight up into the hard palate.

4. Focus on blending the OH vowel into each note.

5. Try not to let go of the thyroid effort when moving from note to note. Focus on not fading off the last note of the scale.

6. The tongue should remain forward, and your volume consistent throughout the scales.

PLAY TRACK #9

The OO Vowel Using the "Red Voice"

The last vowel of this exercise will be OO. Your lips will help to form this vowel correctly, and your jaw will be dropped slightly. This vowel should be enunciated like the word "ew"—the sound you make when you're grossed out. That's how big we want this OO vowel to sound. (Refer to picture #5, Vowel Formation.)

1. Place your fingers on the front of your larynx.

2. As soon as you feel the cold spot, start singing the first note. Use your lips to help form the OO vowel.

3. The air of the OO vowel will be in the back of the hard palate, even though you may feel vibrations more on your lips.

4. Focus on blending the OO vowel into each note.

5. The tongue should remain forward, and your volume should remain consistent throughout the scales.

PLAY TRACK #10

2-Note Scales

If you've conquered the half-step scales, then it's time to work on the 2-note scales. This exercise requires significant movement from the vocal cords, so the thyroid effort is working to stretch them. The first and second note are 2 1/2 steps apart. When exercising with the 2-note scales, place your fingertips on each side of the thyroid cartilage, because the physical movements and vibrations are perceptible by touch. Both notes should be sung equally strong, so resist adding any extra volume during this exercise. Also, when descending from the first to the second note, you should not hear more of a breathier voice. A breathier tone is an indication that you're letting go of the thyroid effort. When the vocal cords are not stretched properly, air can escape between them, causing a breathy voice quality. Start by singing the easier sections of the scales first, then progress to the more challenging areas.

The 2-note scales will start at B-1, descend to F-1, and end on B-1.

2-note scales

The EH Vowel Using the "Red Voice"

When singing the EH vowel, drop the jaw slightly more than when singing the E vowel. (Refer to picture #2, Vowel Formation.)

1. Place your fingers on the front of your larynx.

2. As soon as you feel the cold spot, start singing the first note.

3. Lean the air of the EH vowel into the hard palate. Focus on keeping the air on the hard palate when moving from note to note.

4. Do not sing staccato. Blend the EH vowel into each note. Keep in mind that the EH vowel should not be swelling in and out.

5. Focus on not fading off of your last note of the scale, making it as strong as the first note. If you hear yourself sliding off of the last note, correct yourself. This is a bad habit when executing scales.

6. The EH vowel on the second note should be sung as AA, not AE. This means the E sound should not be enunciated on the ending note. Listen to the CD example as a reference.

PLAY TRACK #11

The E Vowel Using the "Red Voice"

Allow your jaw to relax and slightly drop. You don't want to have tension in your jaw, or else you'll have a tight sounding E vowel. Remember to form a big E sound; the E should feel almost as big as the EH vowel. (Refer to picture #1, Vowel Formation.)

1. Place your fingers on the front of your larynx.

2. As soon as you feel the cold spot, start singing your first note.

3. Place the air of the E vowel as far forward in your hard palate as you can. Try and keep a slight smile on your most difficult notes in the lower section of the "Red Voice."

4. The tongue should remain forward throughout the entire exercise.

5. Do not sing staccato or add vibrato to either note.

6. Blend the E vowel from the starting note into the second note.

7. Focus on not fading off the second note.

PLAY TRACK #12

The AH Vowel Using the "Red Voice"

When singing the AH vowel, drop the jaw slightly more than when singing the EH vowel. (Refer to picture #3, Vocal Formation.)

1. Place your fingers on the front of your larynx.

2. As soon as you feel the cold spot, start singing your first note.

3. Check and see if you are blending the AH vowel into both notes. The breath of the AH vowel should be placed right behind the breath of the EH vowel in the hard palate, towards the center. Keep this placement throughout the entire exercise. A common bad habit is to move its placement back while descending the scale.

4. Check that your tongue remains forward throughout the scales.

5. Do not sing staccato or add vibrato to either note.

6. Focus on not fading off the second note.

PLAY TRACK #13

The OH Vowel Using the "Red Voice"

The jaw may be dropped in the same manner as the AH vowel. Your lips will help you form this vowel properly. (Refer to picture #4, Vowel Formation.)

1. Place your fingers on the front of your larynx.

2. As soon as you feel the cold spot, start singing your first note.

3. Focus on engaging an OH sound on the first note. If you are having difficulty placing the air of the OH vowel forward in the hard palate, place an "h" sound in front of the OH vowel. Pulse on the word "ho," quickly shooting the air straight up into the hard palate.

4. Focus on blending the OH vowel into each note.

5. Try not to let go of the thyroid effort when moving from note to note. Focus on not fading off the last note of the scale.

6. The tongue should remain forward, and your volume should remain consistent throughout the scales.

PLAY TRACK #14

The OO Vowel Using the "Red Voice"

The last vowel in this exercise will be the OO vowel. Your lips will help to form this vowel correctly, and your jaw will be dropped slightly. This vowel should be enunciated like the word "ew"—the sound you make when you're grossed out. That's how big we want this OO vowel to sound. (Refer to picture #5, Vowel Formation.)

1. Place your fingers on the front of your larynx.

2. As soon as you feel the cold spot, start singing the first note. Use your lips to help form the OO vowel.

3. Air of the OO vowel will be in the back of the hard palate, even though you may feel vibrations more on your lips.

4. Focus on blending the OO vowel into each note.

5. The tongue should remain forward, and your volume should remain consistent throughout the scales.

PLAY TRACK#15

Chapter Four
ENGAGING THE "BLUE VOICE" (UPPER REGISTER)

When singing these scales, it is also important to focus on specific sensations and sounds. The physical sensations of the arytenoid effort are very different from the thyroid effort. The arytenoid movements are more delicate and subtle in comparison. Keeping a relaxed and open throat will make it easier to physically feel the arytenoids and vocal cord movements.

The first thing we need to do when singing in the upper register is to isolate the back inner edges of the vocal cords. Using a *head voice* (falsetto) will help develop this stretch correctly. If the vocal cords are pushed with too much air pressure, volume, or muscle tension, an incorrect development can be established and serious damage can result. Through my years of experience working with many rock vocalists, one or a combination of these bad habits have been a factor in an uncontrolled upper register. Many vocalists associate a head voice with an airy, breathy, weak, or wimpy sound. The head voice's tone should sound controlled and strong, not unlike the chest voice's full tone. When all vowels have been sung with correct production, we can start adding more weight to the vocal cords. This will occur mostly in the top-middle register (around A+1 to C+1) to the lower-middle register (around middle C to G+1). After strengthening the upper register, we will move on to developing a stronger voice overall. We'll develop the areas of the back inner edges, the middle layer, as well as a stronger engagement from the vocal cords (this is the weight I previously mentioned) needed to produce this fuller-sounding voice. We'll also need a combination of the mask and chest resonance to fill out the vocal tone. These note ranges I speak of are average estimates I've seen with students, but everyone is different. The upper register is definitely a tricky technique to master. But if exercised with focus and precision, the upper register will come much easier.

Training the upper register is slightly more difficult for two reasons: (1) The movements of the arytenoids and vocal cords are subtle, and (2) you can't see how the voice should be positioned for each note. Once again, you must visualize and feel the movements and sensations while singing, and, of course, develop your ears to distinguish the best sounds. When singing in the upper register, the tone of the voice should be light, thin, and bright. I call this your "Blue Voice."

When singing these scales, it is important to focus on particular sensations and sounds. At first, you'll be thinking a lot when singing these scales. Remember, you're exercising the vocal cords and their mechanisms, and developing muscle memory. As you progress, this type of concentration won't be as necessary when practicing or performing.

2-Note Scales

For some, focusing on the 2-note scales might sound simple, but it can be complicated for those who prominently sing in the lower register or have difficulty singing in the upper register. Singers that like to push with volume and air pressure will normally experience tension. It may feel as if there is no hope to achieve this register, but that's a very common misconception. I like to call this the "hope and wish" scenario: You cross your fingers and hope and wish that you hit the high note in your song. It's now time to say goodbye to that!

Here is an important fact to remember: If your first two notes of the scale are not solid, whatever notes that follow will more than likely be weak. You need to correctly stretch the vocal cords to have consistent control throughout the scales that are sung. How many of you have come in to sing the first few words of a song and were a little off pitch? You should be able to fix the problem, but for some, panic sets in, making it difficult to adjust back into the correct pitch. With the 2-note scales, we're basically working the foundation of your upper register, so we can build the precision and accuracy needed.

During the 2-note scale movements, the arytenoid effort can be felt when singing from the first to the second note (2 1/2 steps down). Focus on the area behind the thyroid cartilage (that's where the arytenoids are). Unfortunately, we can't simply place our fingers there to feel this vibration, as with the thyroid effort, because they're inside the throat. When starting this exercise, focus on a slight drop from the first to the second note inside the larynx. Also, notice that the first note causes your arytenoid effort to lift a little. Sing all the vowels consecutively for each scale.

Listen first to the vocal example as a reference point, then sing on the repeat.

2-note scales start at G+1, ascend to the note G+2, and return to G+1.

etc.

The E, EH, AH, OH, and OO Vowels Using the "Blue Voice"

We'll start the 2-note scales with the E vowel. The E vowel sound should feel big inside the mouth—not tight and small, because that closes the throat. After that, sing the EH, AH, OH, and OO vowels.

It's important to focus on engaging each vowel sound when starting the first note of the 2-note scales. I'll use the term "hooking." That means to engage the starting note with the vowel and land solidly on it! When descending to the second note, maintain that vowel sound. A common mistake with the second note is to let go of the vowel sound, which makes the arytenoid effort to let go of the stretch of the vocal cords, resulting in an airy quality.

1. Place your finger on your Adam's Apple. It should remain still while singing the 2-note scale. If it jumps up (as if when swallowing), then this is an indication that you're letting go of the stretch of the vocal cords or pushing with air pressure. The Adam's Apple will *slightly* move upwards while singing (in the top section of your "Blue Voice"), but it's very subtle.

2. As soon as you feel the cold spot, start singing the first note. Each vowel sound should have its own individual breath support. If you are experiencing a tight throat, place both hands on each side of it and take a breath. The throat will expand, and as soon as you feel the cold spot, start to sing the first note and keep the throat expanded until completing the last note sung.

3. Engage the vowel sound and "hook" the starting note. Descend with the vowel sound into the second note. Focus on the arytenoid effort and vocal cord movements from the starting note to the second note. (Refer to pictures 1–5 in the Vowel Formation chapter.)

4. Lean the air placement of *each* vowel in your hard palate.

5. Do not use vibrato when exercising the 2-note scales.

6. Check to see that your tongue remains forward and that your volume is consistent throughout the scales.

PLAY TRACK #16

5-Note Scales

The 5-note scales can be more of a challenge to conquer than the 2-note scales, because they require more discipline from the arytenoids. When singing them, try to remain in the head voice. Remember: The point of this exercise is to strengthen the back inner edges of the vocal cords. The head voice cannot withstand any excessive amount of air pressure, because the voice will crack, flip into the chest voice, or sound tight. Once the vocal cords are strengthened and all vowels have been exercised, it will be easier to begin filling out the upper register's tone. While producing some of these notes, particularly in the lower-upper register, there will be a tendency to want to fill out the tone by adding in the mixed or chest voice. Stay consistent with the head voice for now.

When exercising the 5-note scales, the voice will be moving from the first to the second note by 2 1/2 steps down; the second to the third note is a whole step up; the third to the fourth note is 2 steps down; and the fourth to the fifth note is a whole step up. During this exercise you should be able to really feel the arytenoid movements, and the more you focus, the more you will be able to train the muscle memory of your upper register. When singing the first two notes, see if you can feel a slight drop in the area behind the thyroid. If you can feel it, pay attention to what happens from note-to-note: From the second to the third, a slight raise; from the third to the fourth, a slight drop; and lastly, a slight lift from the fourth to the final note. As we move into the upper register, you may begin feeling an up-and-back stretch to the first note; this is a good sign. When you're not speaking or singing, the vocal cords are in a relaxed state, but when the vocal cords engage the upper register, you can feel it, as long as you remain relaxed.

Place your finger on the Adam's Apple. As said before, the Adam's Apple should remain still when singing the 5-note scales, but if it moves as if you're swallowing (as you sing) it's an indication that you're letting go of the stretch of the vocal cords or pushing air. The Adam's Apple does move slightly upwards (in the top section of your "Blue Voice"), but it's very subtle.

Note: Remember, we are not going for power, loudness, or strength right now, so don't worry if your tone is soft or weak. Also, you might not be able to sing all of these scales at first, which is completely normal! You are probably exercising areas of your voice that haven't used before. Start by singing the easier sections of the scales first, then progress to more challenging areas. Your voice will appreciate your patience.

Listen first to the vocal example as a reference point, then sing on the repeat.

The 5-note scales will start at A+1, ascend to C+2, and then descend to A+1.

The E Vowel Using the "Blue Voice"

1. Place your finger on the Adam's Apple to check that your larynx is not rising while singing.

2. As soon as you feel the cold spot, start singing your first note.

3. Quickly "hook" the note, then move along the exercise while keeping the E vowel engaged. The E vowel should not sound small or feel tight, but almost as big as the EH vowel.

4. You should feel a lift from the arytenoids stretching the vocal cords. The higher we sing in the "Blue Voice," the more we'll feel the lift and stretching. Picture a slingshot stretching up and back, but never letting go!

5. Keep the throat open and relaxed throughout the 5-note scales. It's a good idea to keep your hands on both sides of your throat as a reference point.

6. For the higher notes, the inner part of the mouth needs to be more elongated.

7. Make sure the air of the E vowel is leaning correctly into the hard palate.

8. Your mouth should have a slight smile. This will help to form the E vowel and help brighten the tone. This will be especially important on the fourth and fifth notes of the scale.

9. Do not add staccato, vibrato, volume, or swell in and out while singing the 5-note scales.

10. Check to see that your tongue remains forward while keeping a consistent volume throughout the scale.

11. When finished singing the fifth note of the scales, simply end the sung note. If you let go of the arytenoid effort while still singing, the voice can crack/break.

PLAY TRACK #17

The EH Vowel Using the "Blue Voice"

The EH vowel in the "Blue Voice" has a very similar stretch to the E vowel, but it's slightly more open. Many singers make the mistake of opening their mouths too wide, so, instead focus more on the stretch of your vocal cords. If you still have a problem with the EH vowel, try starting on an E vowel and quickly move to the EH. This method works because you have already developed the muscle memory for the E vowel, and moving from there to the EH vowel is easier. The air of the EH vowel should be leaned slightly behind the E in the hard palate, but avoid sliding it back from there.

1. Place your finger on the Adam's Apple to check that your larynx is not rising up when singing the scales.

2. As soon as you feel the cold spot, start singing your first note.

3. "Hook" the note quickly, then move from note to note while keeping the EH vowel engaged.

4. You should feel a lift from the arytenoids stretching the vocal cords. The higher we sing in the "Blue Voice," the more we'll feel the stretching of the arytenoids and vocal cords.

5. Keep the throat open and relaxed throughout the scales. You can place your hands on both sides of your throat as a reference point.

6. For the higher notes of the scales, the inner part of the mouth needs to be more elongated.

7. Make sure the air of the EH vowel is leaned correctly into the hard palate.

8. Do not use staccato, vibrato, volume, or swell in and out while singing the 5-note scales.

9. Check to see that your tongue remains forward throughout.

10. When finished singing the fifth note of the scales, simply end the sung note.

PLAY TRACK #18

The AH Vowel Using the "Blue Voice"

A mistake with the AH is overcompensating its formation, where the jaw drops, leaving the mouth too wide open. Think on a physical level; putting your finger on the Adam's Apple when you start engaging the AH vowel sound helps ensure that it doesn't raise. The AH vowel can be challenging around the fourth and fifth notes, so try and keep your focus. If you are having difficulty, work up to it by starting with the E and EH vowels

1. Place your finger on the Adam's Apple to check that your larynx is not rising up when singing the scales.

2. As soon as you feel the cold spot, start singing your first note.

3. "Hook" the note quickly, then move from note to note while keeping the AH vowel engaged.

4. You should feel a lift from the arytenoids, stretching the vocal cords.

5. Keep the throat open and relaxed throughout the scales. You can place your hands on both sides of your throat as a reference point.

6. For the higher notes of the scale, the inner part of the mouth needs to be more elongated.

7. Make sure the air of the AH vowel is leaned correctly into the hard palate.

8. Do not use staccato, vibrato, or swell in and out while singing the 5-note scales.

9. Check to see that your tongue remains forward and your volume consistent throughout.

10. When finished singing the fifth note of the scales, simply end the sung note.

PLAY TRACK #19

The OH Vowel Using the "Blue Voice"

The OH vowel must also have a strong emphasis on engaging the arytenoid effort right away. A common problem with this vowel is with the tongue sliding back, so keep it touching the bottom-front row of your teeth. The air of the OH vowel is right behind the AH vowel, so it's near the back of the hard palate. It seems easier to sing through these scales by focusing on keeping that resonance through each note. The OH sounds hollow, but not as hollow as the OO vowel.

1. Place your finger on the Adam's Apple to check that your larynx is not rising up when singing the scales.

2. As soon as you feel the cold spot, start singing your first note.

3. "Hook" the note quickly, then move from note to note while keeping the OH vowel engaged.

4. You should feel a lift from the arytenoids, stretching the vocal cords.

5. Keep the throat open and relaxed throughout the scales. You can place your hands on both sides of your throat as a reference point.

6. For the higher notes of the scales, the inner part of the mouth needs to be more elongated.

7. Make sure the air of the OH vowel is leaned correctly into the hard palate.

8. Do not use staccato, vibrato, or swell in and out while singing the scales.

9. Check to see that your tongue remains forward and your volume consistent throughout.

10. When finished singing the fifth note of the scales, simply end the sung note.

PLAY TRACK #20

The OO Vowel Using the "Blue Voice"

The OO vowel is much easier to produce correctly than E, EH or AH vowels for those vocalists who have muscle tension in the upper register. The OO is known as one of the "air vowels," because the vocal cords allow a little more air to pass through them. The sound of OO is leaned straight up into the hard palate. Using the lips (almost puckered) will help to form the OO correctly. It should sound resonant and hollow. As mentioned before, if you notice that your lips are shaking, relax the lips a little more. If you're still having trouble, gently press your fingers on the corners of your mouth to stop the trembling while singing.

1. Place your finger on the Adam's Apple to check that your larynx is not rising up when singing the scales.

2. As soon as you feel the cold spot, start singing your first note.

3. "Hook" the note quickly, then move from note to note while keeping the OO vowel engaged.

4. You should feel a lift from the arytenoids, stretching the vocal cords.

5. Keep the throat open and relaxed throughout the scales. You can place your hands on both sides of your throat as a reference point.

6. For the higher notes of the scales, the inner part of the mouth needs to be more elongated.

7. Make sure the air of the OO vowel is leaned correctly into the hard palate.

8. Do not use staccato, vibrato, or swell in and out while singing the scales.

9. Check to see that your tongue remains forward and volume consistent throughout.

10. When finished singing the fifth note of the scales, simply end the vowel sounds.

PLAY TRACK #21

Chapter Five
SINGING IN THE MIDDLE REGISTER

5

Singing in the middle register is probably one of the most misunderstood and difficult areas to execute smoothly. It is also the most important area to control, because ninety percent of rock music is sung in the middle register. The remaining ten percent is typically sung in the upper register.

The middle register, for the majority of singers, has some notes that are easy to sing and others that are more difficult to control. This means that singers tend to be unsure when to switch from chest to head voice for difficult notes. Additionally, singers have trouble with the voice cracking in this area. I haven't met a vocalist yet that hasn't had this problem (including myself). Remember, you should always have full control of the middle register. If you want to sing with a chest, falsetto or mixed voice, you should be able to not only produce it, but also control it. Maintaining a dynamic voice requires a wide range of vocal abilities.

I bet you're thinking, "Why didn't we learn this at the beginning, since this is so useful in real-life situations?" Well, the arytenoids and thyroids must become equally strong to handle the transitions from the middle to lower and upper registers.

Mask Resonance

In this area of study, we are working to shift head resonance into the *mask*. This resonance occurs in your sinus cavities, and it is vital for bridging the middle (chest voice) to the upper register. The sound in the mask is a much fuller tone than the head, but we're not using any extra volume or air pressure to achieve this. It's a purely natural, powerful resonating tone that is produced. A common related question is, "Are you talking about a nasal sounding tone?" No! A nasal tone is closed off and usually, I must say, annoying.

Another important factor in mask resonance is the arytenoids, because they stretch the vocal cords. If you have been working on your "Blue Voice" correctly, you should be ready to move on to resonating in the mask. The areas of the vocal cords that are being used in this production are the back, inner edges, and middle layers of your vocal cords. Sometimes singers think that there must be some special way the vocal cords work in the middle register, but there isn't. The only two unique things are the slightly stronger engagement of the arytenoid effort and the dilation of the nose. Look in the mirror and gently squint your nose, showing your two front teeth—focus on the throat remaining open as well. Physically, what happens when you squint is that the soft palate and uvula are pulling forward. This leaves an open passageway for the sound to travel up into the nasopharynx, so when you engage the arytenoids (stretching your vocal cords) it helps direct resonance to your mask.

If you're having difficulty, try using the sounds "nee," "neh," "nah," "noh," and "noo." Open the mouth to help form the vowel sound. The "n" is a nasal sound that can help set a reference point for your mask resonance. Speaking with mask resonance produces bright, forward, and balanced tone—not thin and nasal sounding!

This exercise will require an isolation of mask resonance when blending all the vowels into each individual note. We will sing each note starting with the E, blending into EH, AH, OH, and finally the OO vowels. The most challenging part is maintaining a smooth transition from vowel to vowel. Each note needs to be equally strong to assure a smooth, consistent flow when moving from the middle to upper register. This is an area where vocalists have met some frustration, and it's become known as the "vocal break." The biggest mistake you can make is to push through with either pressure of breath or volume to hit the note.

Note: Once again, we are not going for power, loudness, or strength right now. You might produce a very soft or weak tone at first. Don't panic! Your voice will strengthen and become much fuller as time goes on. A common question I am asked is: "How long before these exercises improve my tone?" Regardless of the current strength of your tone, you will hear *and* feel an improvement in a very short time. For beginners, you most likely will have an underdeveloped tone, but you will see marked improvement very quickly using this exercise. Also, you might not be able to sing all of these scales at first, which is completely normal! Remember, you are probably exercising areas of your voice that haven't been exercised before. Start by singing the easier sections first, then progress to more challenging areas. Your voice will appreciate your patience.

Listen first to the vocal example as a reference point, then sing on the repeat.

The mask resonance exercise starts at C+1, descends by half steps to A♭+1, ascends to E+2, and returns to C+1.

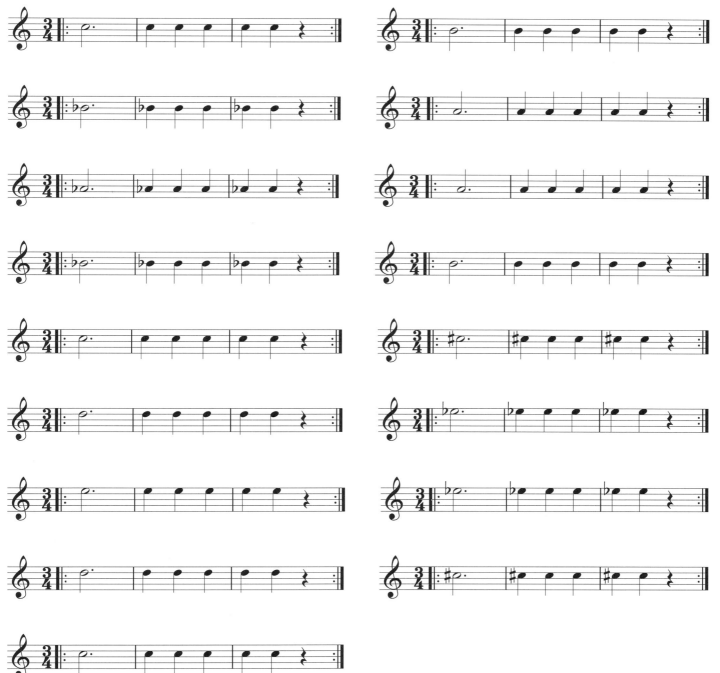

All Vowels Using Mask Resonance

1. Place your finger on the Adam's Apple to check that your larynx is not rising up when singing during the exercise.

2. Keep your nose dilated *and* the back of the oropharynx open throughout!

3. As soon as you feel the cold spot, quickly "hook" the starting note with the E vowel. While keeping the vocal cords stretched, blend each vowel sound into one another. (Sometimes singers will manipulate the stretch in an attempt to produce the right vowel sound.)

4. Lean the air placement of *each* vowel in your hard palate.

5. Keep the mask resonance equally as strong for each vowel.

6. Check to see that your tongue remains forward and that your volume's consistent throughout.

PLAY TRACK #22

Other Exercises

If you're not sure you're doing this correctly, sit with a keyboard and try singing one note with the E vowel, using head resonance (falsetto). Then try singing the note with mask resonance. Sing in half steps, starting at D+2, down to A♭+1, up to E+2, and back down to D+2. Each note needs to be equally strong to assure a smooth, consistent flow when moving from the middle to upper register.

Focus on not closing the back of the pharynx and throat areas, or else you'll feel an uncomfortable pinch. Typically, the easiest vowels to practice with mask resonance are the E and OO vowels. You can then bridge the E to the EH vowel, and the OO to the OH vowel. Eventually, bridge all of the vowels in this order: E–EH–AH– OH–OO. It will take patience when bridging both the mask resonance and the "Vendor Voice" together. You are probably not going to be able to successfully make this transition to a smooth "Vendor Voice" at first. It takes time to isolate both these areas, because it's a slow process to build vocal strength.

"Vendor Voice"

The second exercise we're going to use in the middle register uses the "Vendor Voice" exclusively. Just like a vendor's voice at a baseball game or park, the sound is very distinct: projecting, but not screaming or shouting. It cuts through and gets the attention of those around, sounding as if there's a built-in megaphone to the voice. The "Vendor Voice" is also known as a chest voice of the lower-middle register.

The first exercise is spoken. Speaking in the "Vendor Voice" can be tricky, and there are many steps needed to take before we sing in this register. The front, back, inner edges and middle layers of the vocal cords are used when producing a strong "Vendor Voice." To build this kind of vocal strength, a focused regimen of slow conditioning is required, until you can withstand holding notes or singing an entire chorus. The "Vendor Voice" has also been called "belting" and a "full chest voice."

The higher we go in the middle register, the more you must shave off a layer of thickness to our voice. A common bad habit is to add a fuller tone when ascending to the high notes of the middle register. Make sure you stay alert and don't increase your volume or power to help keep a heavy-sounding chest voice.

The heavier you try to make your voice (full tone, chest voice, etc.), the more unnatural your vocal production will be. To put it another way: the higher the note, the lighter in weight the vocal tone must become. You should not sound head-voiced, but you should sound just a little thinner than the bottom note (B-1) of this register. There's a point where the arytenoids are doing most of the vocal work. So halfway through the middle register, when you begin to thin out your voice, start using combined chest and mask resonance (*mixed voice*). As you ascend into the top-middle register, lean a little more into the mask area. The tone of the voice will remain full sounding.

In the beginning, it's common that many vocalists are only able to sing between the notes of F+1 and A+1. Usually around B♭+1 to C+2, there is a point where you will have to use a lighter-sounding "Vendor Voice," while at the same time using mask resonance to help fill out the tone. This area of the middle register is called *bridging*. When you start practicing this, you may sound a little weak. Take your time and you will hear *and* feel results, as long as you are patient and in control of your voice: it will eventually begin to fill out and strengthen in tone.

We will use the word "hey" for the EH vowel and "hoh" for the OH vowel. The "h" sound is helpful, because it allows a little air to pass through the vocal cords before the vowel sound is produced. This will help the voice to project out quickly. Usually one of these vowels is easier to pop out than the other. It's different with every vocalist, so start with one that is easiest to produce. Work on the other vowels after you're comfortable with this production, because you will eventually want to add in all the vowels.

An important thing to focus on is keeping the back of the pharynx open. Imagine the pharynx expanding as it opens up, so you can instantly pop the vowel out in front. Be careful if you are feeling a pinch in the back of the throat, though. It's likely that you're closing off the back of the throat. Placing your fingers on each side of the throat helps to remind staying open after taking in a breath.

Listen first to the vocal example as a reference point, then sing on the repeat.

The "Vendor Voice" exercise starts at B-1, ascending in half steps to C+1, and then returns to the starting note B-1.

Vendor Voice Exercise

The EH and OH Vowels Using the "Vendor Voice"

Approaching this register takes patience. More than likely you won't be able to immediately go through the entire exercise. Go through these notes with full focus on each individual note. Start by going up four notes, down two, up two, and back down one. Stop and take a break for a few seconds between each exercise.

Note: Listen to the silence around you. Sometimes there is a tendency to add volume and air pressure to notes when getting the hang of this exercise. Resist and remain as relaxed as possible. Equally important is developing the muscle memory needed. Take a few seconds in between each exercise. This can be difficult, especially when you're halfway through the middle register. Start off with practicing this area for 10 minutes, then build up to 20 minutes (where you go through this exercise twice).

1. Place your finger on the Adam's Apple to check that your larynx is not rising up when singing the exercise.

2. As soon as you feel the cold spot, quickly "hook" the starting note with the words "hey" and "ho." It should sound as though you're trying to get someone's attention from across the room.

3. Remember to stay relaxed and *not pushed*—no shouting or yelling!

4. Check to make sure the diaphragm is supporting each individual "hey" and "ho."

5. Lean the air placement of *each* vowel in your hard palate.

6. Check to see that your tongue remains forward throughout.

7. In the higher notes of this exercise, the voice needs to have a combination of chest and mask resonance. The chest voice may need to be lighter in tone at first.

PLAY TRACK #23

Mixed Voice

The sound of the *mixed voice* is lighter than the chest voice, but it's heavier than the head voice. The mixed voice will also be referred to as a "voicing". As with the "Vendor Voice," the arytenoids stretch the vocal cords the majority of the time. The thyroid plays an important role in the lower section of the mixed voice. The common range can start at B-1 up to C+1 in the middle register. Resonance for the mixed voice usually occurs with a combination of these locations (chest with mask resonance, mask with head resonance, etc.). For example, think of a car. The sound of the mixed voice can be described in three sections: soft (2nd gear), medium (3rd gear), full (4th gear), and chest (5th gear).

Falsetto/Head Voice (1st Gear): Although this isn't technically a mixed voice, it represents the starting point from where mixed voices are combined. The head voice is a light tone with resonance occurring in the head cavity, engaged by the arytenoids.

Soft Mixed Voice (2nd Gear): A soft mixed voice is light in vocal tone, but not as soft as the head voice. Resonance is primarily occurring in the mask, combined with the head voice, and engaged by the arytenoids.

Medium Mixed Voice (3rd Gear): A medium mixed voice is between the full and soft mixed voicings. Resonance will be more in the mask area, slightly resonating in chest, and engaged by the arytenoids.

Full Mixed Voice (4th Gear): A full mixed voice is just that: the fullest of all mixed voice tones. This voicing resonates in the chest and mask areas, engaged by the thyroid effort in the lower section and by the arytenoid effort for the remainder of the middle register.

Chest Voice (5th Gear): A chest voice is a strong, powerful voice. The thyroid is primarily engaged, with resonance occurring in the chest cavity. Mask resonance can also be applied with the combination of chest resonance. Other names associated with the chest voice are "Vendor Voice" and "belting."

Vocalists who have developed a powerful chest voice but a weak head voice will find the mixed voice very difficult to control. The physical production of the mixed voice occurs at the back inner edges and middle layers of the vocal cords. Vocalists with a solid head voice usually develop the mixed voice much faster. If this voice is pushed by air pressure, squeezed by muscle tension, and/or pushed with excess volume, it will seem impossible to control. Any of these problems will result in a voice sounding forced and unnatural.

The mixed voice is most often used in various sections of songs (verse, pre-chorus, chorus, and bridge), because the mixed voice is the main contributor to a song's *dynamics* (how loud or soft music should be). When singing a song that goes from soft to loud, a smooth transition is needed, calling for the mixed voices to smoothly cross the dynamic gap. This takes a lot of vocal control, and if the mixed voice is not developed, the voice may only be capable of the 1st and 5th gear voices, greatly limiting the dynamics of the song.

When starting to exercise the mixed voice, try using a medium to full sound. If you are not sure how to produce this, refer to the tone and volume of the demo track. In time you will be able to distinguish between, and control, a soft mixed voice (2nd Gear), medium mixed voice (3rd Gear), and full mixed voice (4th Gear). This is very difficult and may take some time to develop complete control.

Place your finger on the Adam's Apple. As said before, the Adam's Apple should remain still while blending all vowels for each note sung. But if it feels as if you're swallowing (as you sing), it's an indication that you're letting go of the stretch of the vocal cords or pushing with air pressure. The Adam's Apple does move slightly upwards (in the top section of your "Blue Voice"), but it's very subtle.

Listen first to the vocal example as a reference point, then sing on the repeat.

The mixed voice exercise starts on A-1 and moves up and down the first five notes of a major scale. The exercise then moves up a half step and starts the next mixed-voice scale. The last starting note of this exercise is G+1, after which we descend to the starting note A-1.

Mixed Voice Exercise

The EH Vowel Using the Mixed Voice

1. Place your finger on the Adam's Apple to check that your larynx is not rising when singing the scales.

2. As soon as you feel the cold spot, start singing your first note.

3. "Hook" the note quickly, then smoothly move from note to note without any interruption in sound.

4. Keep the throat open and relaxed throughout the scales. You can place your hands on the sides of your throat so you can feel that you're keeping the throat open throughout the scales.

5. For the higher section of the mixed-voice scales, the inner part of the mouth needs to be more elongated. A softer combination of chest and mask resonance is also necessary.

6. Make sure the air of the EH vowel is leaned correctly into the hard palate throughout.

7. Do not sing staccato or use vibrato during the mixed-voice scales.

8. Check to see that your tongue remains forward and that your volume's consistent throughout the scale, especially in the higher section.

PLAY TRACK #24

The AH Vowel Using the Mixed Voice

1. Follow all the instructions for the EH vowel, but substitute the AH vowel.

PLAY TRACK #25

The OH Vowel Using the Mixed Voice

1. Follow all the instructions for the EH vowel, but substitute the OH vowel.

PLAY TRACK #26

Chapter Six

6 TIME MANAGEMENT FOR PRACTICE

By now you should be aware of your strong and weak areas, so dedicate more time for practicing the weaker points. But remember, you still must practice all areas: lower register (thyroid effort), upper register (arytenoid effort), and middle register. If you only practice one area all the time, the voice will become unbalanced—remember the gym example? Below are some guidelines to follow when practicing your voice.

The most common question regarding vocal exercises is: "How long should I practice?" Every vocalist has certain exercises and registers that need more focus than others. If your voice has already adapted well to the lower register scales, the upper and middle registers should be the focus of your warm ups. If you need work on the "Red" and "Blue" voices, holding off on the middle register exercises would be a good idea. Listed below is information regarding common practice durations for exercising your voice. The suggested time lengths vary for each level of student. Sometimes the suggested time lengths listed will be less than the CD example. This is because not every vocalist can go through the entire scale. Practice within the areas that you can successfully complete.

"Red Voice" Exercises

Beginners (Struggling):

Start off with a 5 minute warm up in the lower register using the 4 half-step scales. Practice your easiest vowel first, then eventually work in all of them. Each vowel for the 4 half-step scales is a minute long, but if you're having trouble getting through it, practice the areas that you can successfully execute. Slowly exercise and strengthen the voice needed to handle the entire exercise. After successfully completing it, move on to the intermediate practice.

Intermediate (Good Control):

Start off with a 10–15 minute warm up in the lower register using the 2-note scales. Practice your easiest vowel first, then eventually work in all of them. Each vowel for the 2-note scales is 1:24. Practice the areas that you can, but eventually you will be to handle the entire range. If you have a wide range in your upper register, you may not reach the lowest note in this scale range: everyone's range is different. If you can do only a few vowels with this 2-note scale, try working in the other vowels using the 4 half-step scales. Eventually work in all the vowels using the 2-note scale exercise.

Advanced (Perfecting):

Start off with a 15–20 minute warm up in the lower register using the 4-note scales. Practice your easiest vowel first, then eventually work in practicing all of them. Each vowel for the 4-note scales is 3:08. Practice the areas that you can handle. The lowest note in the 4-note scale is E-2, but if you're not able to reach it, sing as low as you can. If some vowels are difficult, try practicing those vowels using the 2-note scale exercise. Eventually work all the vowels into the 4-note scales.

"Blue Voice" Exercises

Beginner to Intermediate:

Start off with a 7–15 minute warm up in the upper register using the 2-note scales. Practice your easiest vowel first, then eventually work in all of them. This scale exercise moves quickly from the E–EH–AH–OH, ending on the OO vowel. Work on what is comfortable, but eventually work in all the vowels. The most important point of this exercise is developing a correct stretch of the vocal cords using the arytenoid effort. The 2-note scales are 6:44, but if you're having trouble getting through them, practice the areas that you can successfully execute. Slowly exercise and strengthen the voice needed to handle the entire scale exercise. After successfully completing this exercise, move on to the intermediate to advanced practice.

Intermediate to Advanced:

Start off with a 15–30 minute warm up in the upper register using the 5-note scales. Practice your easiest vowel first, then eventually work in all of them. This scale exercise moves quickly through the E, EH, AH, OH, and OO vowels. Work on what is comfortable, but eventually work in all the vowels. The most important point of this exercise is developing a correct stretch of the vocal cords using the arytenoid effort.

The 5-note scales are 4:51, with a highest note of C+2. If you're having trouble getting through it, practice to the note that you can successfully execute. Slowly exercise and strengthen the voice needed to handle the entire scale exercise.

Warming up with the 5-note scale is very important before moving on into the other exercises. If your arytenoid effort and vocal cords have not properly warmed up, the "Vendor Voice" and mixed voice exercises will be extremely difficult to execute properly. If you have limited practice time, I suggest at least a 15 minute warm up with the 5-note scales before singing.

Middle Register Exercises

These exercises are divided up into three sections: mask, "Vendor Voice," and mixed voice (for advanced singers). They use the exercises for each voicing, found in Chapter 5. They should only be done once the "Blue Voice" is mastered. Good Luck!

Intermediate to Advanced:

- Mask Resonance: Start off with singing 1–2 times through the mask resonance exercise. It is 3:31, and if you cannot sing the entire range of this exercise, practice the notes you can successfully sing. Also, if blending from vowel to vowel is difficult, sing your easiest vowels first, then eventually work in all of them.

- "Vendor Voice": Start off with singing 1–2 times through with the "Vendor Voice" exercise. It is 3:31, and, once again, only practice the areas that are easy in the beginning. Slowly exercise, and eventually you will be able to complete the entire exercise.

Advanced:

- Mask Resonance: Sing 2–3 times through the mask resonance exercise.

- "Vendor Voice": Sing 2–3 times through the "Vendor Voice" exercise. If some of the higher notes are difficult, sing up to your last successfully completed note. You will eventually be able to sing all the way through it.

- Mixed Voice Scales: Start off with singing once through the mixed voice scale. Practice the notes and vowels you can successfully execute, first—eventually you will be able to do the entire scale. Each individual mixed voice scales are 3:44.

Creating a Practice Log

Keeping a practice log will help you mark your progress, so it is important to keep track of the following:

- What registers to practice?
- What scales to practice?
- What vowels are sung with the different scales?
- How long are you practicing the scales?

You can make your own practice log, or you can photocopy the one below.

VOCAL PRACTICE LOG

REGISTERS PRACTICED: **DATE:**

Lower Register
Scales:_____
Vowels:_____
Length:_____

Upper Register
Scales:_____
Vowels:_____
Length:_____

Middle Register
Scales:_____
Vowels:_____
Length:_____

Chapter Seven
SONG PREPARATION

A common practice method for learning songs is to sing the song over and over again until memorized. This method works for simple songs, but harder songs require a little more focused practicing. Some common challenges in songs include: consonants, range, use of the head, mixed, or chest voice, fast tempo, vocal effects, voice projection, and fatigue.

Consonants

Here are some tips with regard to singing consonants:.

- When a word begins with a "p" or "b," pronounce the sound softer when singing into a microphone. These have a harsh, popping sound that the microphone will pick up and amplify loudly through the P.A. system. Words like "babe," "but," "brave," "pop," "power," and "probably" are good examples to soften the consonant on.
- In the case of contractions, the "t" should be pronounced lightly (i.e., "can't," "won't," etc.).
- When words end with "nd," the "d" sound is often eliminated (i.e., "end," "trend," "lend.")

Vowels

All the vocal exercises we've done up to this point are now going to play an important role when breaking down a song. When singing songs, it's important to emphasize the most open vowels, because melody is carried by them—not consonants. However, vowel sounds are sometimes modified while singing rather than speaking. For example, when speaking, the word "way" is pronounced "waye-ee." But when singing this word on one note, it becomes "waye". Below are the vowels and their modifications when breaking down a song. There are more vowel sounds than previously mentioned, though. When singing, you will use the EH, IH, OW, and UH vowels in addition to those you are already familiar with. When singing the EH and IH vowels, lean the air between the E and A vowels of the hard palate. When singing the OW and UH vowels, lean the air between the AH and OH vowels of the hard palate. Here's a pronunciation guide for each vowel we will encounter when singing songs.

Vowel	Key Word
EE	"see"
A	"way"
AH	"bother"
OH	"ho"
OO	"you"
EH	"get"
IH	"bring"
OW	"now"
UH	"thug"

Here is an example of breaking down the vowels in a line of a song: *So you wanna be a rock star.*

We would break it down in the following way:

So	=	OH vowel
you	=	OO vowel
wan-na	=	AH vowel for both syllables
be	=	E vowel
a	=	UH vowel
rock	=	AH vowel
star	=	UH vowel

If you are experiencing difficulty getting through any line of a particular song, break down the vowel sounds (like we just did), then sing the melody line using only the vowel sounds. When you can sing the vowels, add the words back into the melody. Now you should be able to sing through with ease.

High Notes

When working with songs that challenge their vocal range, many singers never realize how important the vowels are. For example, it's not necessarily the case that the high note is difficult to hit. Usually trouble comes from the notes right before the high note. If those vowels are closed, the high note will be even more closed, causing muscle tension.

Head, Mixed, and Chest Voices

The same scenario can happen when trying to use falsetto, mixed, or chest voices. Songs that demand quick changes in voicings can use falsetto, mixed, or chest all in one line! (Bands like Coldplay or Muse are great examples.) It takes control and the proper execution of open vowels to ensure that there's a smooth transition from word to word and from note to note.

Pitch

Pitch is achieved with the correct stretch of the vocal cords, and singing with closed vowels can affect it (for example, closing on a vowel that's being sung in the upper register). A common bad habit is to push the note out to help control it, but too much can force the note sharp. Another scenario is singing with closed vowels, and the swallowing muscles begin to tighten. It becomes difficult for the thyroid and arytenoids to stretch the vocal cords properly. The pitch can be affected and go flat.

Projection

Many singers think it's only about proper breathing to project the voice. It's actually *resonance* that helps to project the voice. Remember, resonance provides the voice with three qualities: volume (power), balanced tone, and sustain. To produce the best resonance, the voice must be correctly executed ie., open vowels and placement of the vowels in the hard palate. Whether singing powerfully or softly, resonance must be established for the voice to project.

Vocal Effects

Vocal effects include vibrato, growls, screams, and whispers/breathy effects. Everyone that has tried to use any of them has, more than likely, struggled maintaining or controlling them. Why? Many singers have taught themselves by listening to CD examples of well-known singers, trying to imitate them. But what they don't realize is that everything you hear can be manipulated in the studio for any desired effect. Vocalists that may sound as if they're screaming their brains out may actually only be using less than half that volume while recording. The vocalist's tone may also sound really thin, but the mix has helped it sound much fuller. Another little-known fact is that the singer may actually be destroying their voice to produce what you're now trying to imitate. Vocal effects can definitely be challenging, but there's always a way to produce them without hurting yourself.

Vocal effects are one of the techniques to employ when practicing songs. For example, a guitarist that wants to learn a Pantera song doesn't go to Guitar Center to buy all the necessary effects pedals for the song first. The guitarist must learn how to play the song, then add in the effects. It's the same with the voice: learn the melody, check to see that you are singing open vowels for the difficult notes, choose what voicings to use, and then add the vocal effects. Sometimes learning a song is so natural that we don't need a step-by-step process. But when a vocalist is having some difficulty executing the song correctly, taking it step by step really helps.

Vibrato

Vibrato is a rapidly repeating fluctuation in pitch that often starts on a primary note and bends a half step flat and then back to the primary note. Some singers naturally produce this effect, while others desperately work at it—everyone wants something they don't have. Vibrato was typically used as a standard vocal must-have in the eighties rock era. Nowadays, you don't hear it as much, but it adds a nice quality to the voice if used sparingly.

To practice vibrato, sing in a comfortable register with your easiest vowel. Apply a very slow vibrato, then slightly quicken until you can reach the desired tempo. Practicing with a metronome works well for faster speeds. The vibrato is often used sustaining the ending notes of phrases in a song. When singing with a microphone, pull it slightly away from your mouth on higher and louder notes. For lower or softer notes, bring the mic closer to your mouth.

Grit, Growls, and Screams

These are the most challenging effects to execute correctly. Once again, many vocalists assume that they must barrel down, squeeze, push, and scream as loud as they can to imitate these effects—*not true!* You should warm up *very well* with scale exercises before practicing these techniques. Choose a comfortable note and vowel to start off with. Slowly and gently use a glottal attack to initiate the note, then go clean toned with no raspy sound, then go back to a raspy tone. When you start to get the hang of this, begin adding a fuller sound to the voice, until eventually bringing this effect into the controlled, powerful sections of your range. The "Vendor Voice" with this effect sounds great. The upper section of the middle register (A+1 to E+2) is the most difficult area to sing with this effect, so try it with a clean tone first to get the correct vocal stretch and resonance you need. Many of you will be primarily leaning into the mask area. Be very careful that you're not pushing with too much air pressure or squeezing while attempting to do these effects. If so, you'll definitely feel sore in the throat as a result of incorrect execution. When singing with a band, bring the microphone close to your mouth to check that it's loud enough to hear whether or not you're straining your voice.

Volume Swells

Every singer uses this technique when adding dynamic emphasis to a song. When practicing volume swells, start singing soft and gradually get louder, or vice versa. Choose a note and vowel that is most comfortable. The most common problem occurs when singers increase air pressure to add volume. Remember, the more pressure on the vocal cords, the more likely the cords can't vibrate its correct number of vibrations for the pitch that's sung. This will also affect the quality of vocal tone. In live situations, bring the microphone close for soft notes, and pull it away when you belt it. Do not tilt the microphone sideways, because off-axis attenuation results and it will not accurately pick up the full tone you want to project.

Whisper/Breathy Effects

When you practice this effect without a microphone often times the effect sounds good. But what many vocalists don't realize is that if you're allowing too much air to come through the vocal cords more air than vocal tone is likely being produced. A microphone will only pick up what the voice is projecting, which in this case is air. Singing with a band will be even more difficult because the microphone will be picking up the airy vocal tone, causing the vocalist to be drowned out by the instruments. The other problem is that if a vocalist does this technique incorrectly repeatedly over a period of time the vocal cords can become damaged. In severe cases one might develop vocal nodules. The best way to practice this effect is to allow a small amount of air to come through the vocal cords so that there is more vocal tone than air. The tone should be 75% voice while the airy/breathy sound should be 25%. A whisper effect involves the same basic vocal production—the only difference is that the vocal production is much quieter. You will need to bring the microphone closer to your mouth when singing with the whisper effect.

Emotion

The emotion of a song is truly what singing/performing is all about! Whether the vocalist is singing an original or cover song, the emotion is what draws in the audience. A vocalist normally writes lyrics about something that has inspired them in their lives. The truth and dedication of the lyrics, and the melody that flows is a feeling of emotion that is energizing the song; This is what the audience feeds off of. When a singer covers a song, it is often because of a feeling that moved them, be it the message of the lyrics, the vocal texture, or the chills and energy the music instills. To apply 100% emotion to a song, you must allow yourself to let go of any worries or doubts about yourself. Common thoughts are: "What if the audience doesn't like my song? What if I look stupid on stage? What should I say in between the songs? What if my voice cracks? What if I forget the lyrics? What if my band messes up?" Filling your head with doubt and worry before a show psyches yourself out of a great performance. Instead, think of how much time you've put into your songs and what inspired you write or sing them in the first place. The object is to tap into that original emotion, that place where you were first inspired to write this song, and if you do, that energy will help deliver a spectacular performance.

Chapter Eight
8 GIG AND REHEARSAL ETIQUETTE

Microphone

Rock bands usually play loudly and powerfully! How do we sing over this madness? Well, you will need to have a great quality microphone, like my favorite: a Shure Beta 58. I find it works great for projecting at any register and volume. The most commonly used among rock vocalists are the Shure Beta 58 and the Shure SM58, so that's a good place to start. I highly suggest that you test out microphones that best fit your voice. I always have mine in carry-on luggage when I tour, because I can never count on the venue to supply the microphone I like to use.

Monitors and P.A.

For rehearsals, it's good to have a P.A. system and a monitor wedge, so you can be heard over your loud, rocking band. But if your band *really* likes to blast, it can be a challenge to compete with their volume. It is a bad sign if you feel tired and sore after a rehearsal or gig, because the next day your voice will be thrashed. Remember: *You can't buy yourself a new pair of vocal cords!* Sometimes we have to remind not only ourselves but the band members as well. At gigs or practice, make sure your microphone is slightly louder than the band, otherwise you risk straining/damaging your voice. Blaming your voice for a bad performance is like saying, "Hi, I have no idea what I'm doing!" This is just an example of real-life scenarios, so learning such real-life lessons will help you become a better singer/performer even faster.

Sound and Line Checks

A *sound check* allows you to check the levels of each member of your band while running through a song or two. Normally the venue will tell you how long you get to sound check. A *line check* is a very short time to check levels of instruments and voice at the same time. Whether you're doing a sound or line check, always play with the loudest volume your band will be at during your gig. Normally the loudest part of your set will be choruses, so be prepared with what song you'll use. The sound person/production staff gets annoyed when bands don't know what to sound check with. They might even cut your allowed time to sound check. Never piss off the production staff; they either can make you sound great or make you sound terrible! Vocalists: Know your sound people by name. They will help you dial in the sound you hear on stage, so remember: even if you are not happy with the mix, always thank the mixer. You never know when you will play the venue again or will be working with him or her in the future. I can't tell you how many times I've seen performers lay into the sound person after the show, only to find that same sound person two weeks later at a different club. The moral of the story: *never* give the sound person a reason to hate you!

Your Future

Following a practice regimen will allow you to see and hear noticeable improvement with your voice. Practicing the scales and applying all the information in this book will help you keep focused on your vocal goals. Think of yourself as a professional vocal athlete: your voice needs continual exercise to stay in the best condition. A professional football player doesn't say, "Yeah, I'm great. I don't need to practice or exercise anymore." Maintaining a singing career in rock takes complete dedication and hard work. If you have that desire and drive, then you will continue to grow and improve. Dedicate yourself to these exercises, and the sky is the limit!

Credits

I dedicate this book to my late father, Grant Sheehan, Sr., who inspired me to become the vocalist I am today. I would also like to thank the following people who have helped me through the process of completing this book/CD: Marianne Sheehan, Grant Sheehan Jr. (many thanks!), Ray Luzier, Ariel Belkin, Daniel White, Mike Campbell, Ellen Kotheimer, Blackie, Faith Jeon, Toshinori Hiketa, and my students, all of whom have been an inspiration and guide throughout my career.

About the Author

Photo by Natalie Bopp

Coreen Sheehan

Coreen Sheehan is originally from Baltimore, Maryland. Currently she writes curriculum for and instructs Vocal Technique, Pro Performance Showcasing, and Teacher Training classes; Rock Vocal and Vocal English workshops; Artist Showcase performances, Accent Reduction, private lessons and open counseling at Musician's Institute of Technology in Hollywood, California. Coreen also wrote vocal technique curriculum and was an advisor and instructor for seven M.I. Japan schools and instructed students at O.S.M. in Osaka, T.C.A. in Tokyo, and F.S.M. in Fukuoka, Japan from 1994-1999. She also taught at T.P.A. in Taipei, Taiwan.

Coreen was hired as a Music Consultant in 2003 for the VH1 television show *You Rock*, for which she prepared vocalists to perform in concert with artists such as Rod Stewart and the Barenaked Ladies. She has also been seen and heard in TV commercials in the U.S., Germany, Japan (MTV), and South Korea.

In 2002, 2003, and from 2005-2007 Coreen was nominated for the Best Rock Vocalist award in Los Angeles. She won the award in 2005, 2006, and 2007.

Coreen has toured professionally all over the world performing in bands such as the all-female AC/DC tribute band, Whole Lotta Rosies, and Tyed Dyed Junkies during her time in Japan. Her bands have opened for David Lee Roth and the Foo Fighters, and she performed background vocals on Richie Kotzen and Richie Zito's upcoming CD *The Road*. She has also performed with the Bricks Dance Company in Paris at the invitation of the Japanese embassy. Coreen continues to work with artists and bands, preparing them to record and perform in the Los Angeles area. For more information, visit **www.coreensheehan.com** .

Musicians Institute Press

is the official series of Southern California's renowned music school, Musicians Institute. **MI** instructors, some of the finest musicians in the world, share their vast knowledge and experience with you – no matter what your current level. For guitar, bass, drums, vocals, and keyboards, **MI Press** offers the finest music curriculum for higher learning through a variety of series:

ESSENTIAL CONCEPTS
Designed from MI core curriculum programs.

MASTER CLASS
Designed from MI elective courses.

PRIVATE LESSONS
Tackle a variety of topics "one-on-one" with MI faculty instructors.

KEYBOARD

Blues Hanon
by Peter Deneff • Private Lessons
00695708 .... $14.95

Dictionary of Keyboard Grooves
by Gail Johnson • Private Lessons
00695556 Book/CD Pack $16.95

Funk Keyboards – The Complete Method
by Gail Johnson • Master Class
00695336 Book/CD Pack $14.95

Jazz Chord Hanon
by Peter Deneff • Private Lessons
00695791 .... $12.95

Jazz Hanon
by Peter Deneff • Private Lessons
00695554 .... $12.95

Jazz Piano
by Christian Klikovits • Essential Concepts
00695773 Book/CD Pack $17.95

Keyboard Technique
by Steve Weingard • Essential Concepts
00695365 .... $12.95

Keyboard Voicings
by Kevin King • Essential Concepts
00695209 .... $12.95

Music Reading for Keyboard
by Larry Steelman • Essential Concepts
00695205 .... $12.95

Pop Rock Keyboards
by Henry Sol-Eh Brewer & David Garfield • Private Lessons
00695509 Book/CD Pack $19.95

R&B Soul Keyboards
by Henry J. Brewer • Private Lessons
00695327 Book/CD Pack $16.95

Rock Hanon
by Peter Deneff • Private Lessons
00695784 .... $12.95

Salsa Hanon
by Peter Deneff • Private Lessons
00695226 .... $12.95

Stride Hanon
by Peter Deneff • Private Lessons
00695882 .... $12.95

DRUM

Afro-Cuban Coordination for Drumset
by Maria Martinez • Private Lessons
00695328 Book/CD Pack $14.95

Blues Drumming
by Ed Roscetti • Essential Concepts
00695623 Book/CD Pack $14.95

Brazilian Coordination for Drumset
by Maria Martinez • Master Class
00695284 Book/CD Pack $14.95

Chart Reading Workbook for Drummers
by Bobby Gabriele • Private Lessons
00695129 Book/CD Pack $14.95

Double Bass Drumming
by Jeff Bowders
00695723 Book/CD Pack $19.95

Drummer's Guide to Odd Meters
by Ed Roscetti • Essential Concepts
00695349 Book/CD Pack $14.95

Funk & Hip-Hop Grooves for Drums
by Ed Roscetti • Private Lessons
00695679 Book/CD Pack $14.95

Latin Soloing for Drumset
by Phil Maturano • Private Lessons
00695287 Book/CD Pack $14.95

Musician's Guide to Recording Drums
by Dallan Beck • Master Class
00695755 Book/CD Pack $19.95

Rock Drumming Workbook
by Ed Roscetti • Private Lessons
00695838 Book/CD Pack $19.95

Working the Inner Clock for Drumset
by Phil Maturano • Private Lessons
00695127 Book/CD Pack $16.95

VOICE

Harmony Vocals
by Mike Campbell & Tracee Lewis • Private Lessons
00695262 Book/CD Pack $17.95

Musician's Guide to Recording Vocals
by Dallan Beck • Private Lessons
00695626 Book/CD Pack $14.95

Sightsinging
by Mike Campbell • Essential Concepts
00695195 .... $17.95

Vocal Technique
by Dena Murray • Essential Concepts
00695427 Book/CD Pack $22.95

OTHER REFERENCE

Approach to Jazz Improvisation
by Dave Pozzi • Private Lessons
00695135 Book/CD Pack $17.95

Ear Training
by Keith Wyatt, Carl Schroeder & Joe Elliott • Essential Concepts
00695198 Book/2-CD Pack $19.95

Encyclopedia of Reading Rhythms
by Gary Hess • Private Lessons
00695145 .... $19.95

Going Pro
by Kenny Kerner • Private Lessons
00695322 .... $17.95

Harmony & Theory
by Keith Wyatt & Carl Schroeder • Essential Concepts
00695161 .... $17.95

Home Recording Basics
featuring Dallan Beck
00695655 VHS Video $19.95

Lead Sheet Bible
by Robin Randall & Janice Peterson • Private Lessons
00695130 Book/CD Pack $19.95

FOR MORE INFORMATION, SEE YOUR LOCAL MUSIC DEALER,
OR WRITE TO:

HAL•LEONARD®
CORPORATION
7777 W. BLUEMOUND RD. P.O. BOX 13819 MILWAUKEE, WI 53213
Visit Hal Leonard Online at **www.halleonard.com**

Prices, contents, and availability subject to change without notice

0705

MUSICIANS INSTITUTE PRESS is the official series of Southern California's renowned music school, Musicians Institute. MI instructors, some of the finest musicians in the world, share their vast knowledge and experience with you – no matter what your current level. For guitar, bass, drums, vocals, and keyboards, MI Press offers the finest music curriculum for higher learning through a variety of series:

ESSENTIAL CONCEPTS
Designed from MI core curriculum programs.

MASTER CLASS
Designed from MI elective courses.

PRIVATE LESSONS
Tackle a variety of topics "one-on one" with MI faculty instructors.

BASS

Arpeggios for Bass
by Dave Keif • Private Lessons
00695133.............................. $14.95

The Art of Walking Bass
by Bob Magnusson • Master Class
00695168 Book/CD Pack $18.95

Bass Fretboard Basics
by Paul Farnen • Essential Concepts
00695201.............................. $16.95

Bass Playing Techniques
by Alexis Sklarevski • Essential Concepts
00695207.............................. $16.95

Chords for Bass
by Dominik Hauser • Master Class
00695934 Book/CD Pack $16.95

Groove Mastery
by Oneida James • Private Lessons
00695771 Book/CD Pack $17.95

Grooves for Electric Bass
by David Keif • Private Lessons
00695265 Book/CD Pack $15.99

Latin Bass
by George Lopez and David Keif • Private Lessons
00695543 Book/CD Pack $15.99

Music Reading for Bass
by Wendy Wrehovcsik • Essential Concepts
00695203.............................. $10.95

GUITAR

Advanced Guitar Soloing
by Daniel Gilbert & Beth Marlis • Essential Concepts
00695636 Book/CD Pack $19.95

Advanced Scale Concepts & Licks for Guitar
by Jean Marc Belkadi • Private Lessons
00695298 Book/CD Pack $16.95

Basic Blues Guitar
by Steve Trovato • Private Lessons
00695180 Book/CD Pack $15.99

Blues/Rock Soloing for Guitar
by Robert Calva • Private Lessons
00695680 Book/CD Pack $18.95

Blues Rhythm Guitar
by Keith Wyatt • Master Class
00695131 Book/CD Pack $19.95

Dean Brown
00696002 DVD...................... $29.95

Chord Progressions for Guitar
by Tom Kolb • Private Lessons
00695664 Book/CD Pack $16.95

Chord Tone Soloing
by Barrett Tagliarino • Private Lessons
00695855 Book/CD Pack $22.95

Chord-Melody Guitar
by Bruce Buckingham • Private Lessons
00695646 Book/CD Pack $16.95

Prices, contents, and availability subject to change without notice.
FOR MORE INFORMATION, SEE YOUR LOCAL MUSIC DEALER,
OR WRITE TO:

7777 W. BLUEMOUND RD. P.O. BOX 13819 MILWAUKEE, WI 53213

www.halleonard.com

Classical & Fingerstyle Guitar Techniques
by David Oakes • Master Class
00695171 Book/CD Pack $16.95

Classical Themes for Electric Guitar
by Jean Marc Belkadi • Private Lessons
00695806 Book/CD Pack $15.99

Contemporary Acoustic Guitar
by Eric Paschal & Steve Trovato • Master Class
00695320 Book/CD Pack $16.95

Creative Chord Shapes
by Jamie Findlay • Private Lessons
00695172 Book/CD Pack $10.99

Diminished Scale for Guitar
by Jean Marc Belkadi • Private Lessons
00695227 Book/CD Pack $10.99

Essential Rhythm Guitar
by Steve Trovato • Private Lessons
00695181 Book/CD Pack $15.99

Ethnic Rhythms for Electric Guitar
by Jean Marc Belkadi • Private Lessons
00695873 Book/CD Pack $17.99

Exotic Scales & Licks for Electric Guitar
by Jean Marc Belkadi • Private Lessons
00695860 Book/CD Pack $16.95

Funk Guitar
by Ross Bolton • Private Lessons
00695419 Book/CD Pack $15.99

Guitar Basics
by Bruce Buckingham • Private Lessons
00695134 Book/CD Pack $17.95

Guitar Fretboard Workbook
by Barrett Tagliarino • Essential Concepts
00695712.............................. $17.99

Guitar Hanon
by Peter Deneff • Private Lessons
00695321.............................. $9.95

Guitar Lick•tionary
by Dave Hill • Private Lessons
00695482 Book/CD Pack $18.95

Guitar Soloing
by Dan Gilbert & Beth Marlis • Essential Concepts
00695190 Book/CD Pack $19.95
00695907 DVD...................... $19.95

Harmonics
by Jamie Findlay • Private Lessons
00695169 Book/CD Pack $13.99

Introduction to Jazz Guitar Soloing
by Joe Elliott • Master Class
00695406 Book/CD Pack $19.95

Jazz Guitar Chord System
by Scott Henderson • Private Lessons
00695291.............................. $10.95

Jazz Guitar Improvisation
by Sid Jacobs • Master Class
00695128 Book/CD Pack $18.99
00695908 DVD...................... $19.95
00695639 VHS Video $19.95

Jazz-Rock Triad Improvising
by Jean Marc Belkadi • Private Lessons
00695361 Book/CD Pack $15.99

Latin Guitar
by Bruce Buckingham • Master Class
00695379 Book/CD Pack $16.95

Modern Approach to Jazz, Rock & Fusion Guitar
by Jean Marc Belkadi • Private Lessons
00695143 Book/CD Pack $15.99

Modern Jazz Concepts for Guitar
by Sid Jacobs • Master Class
00695711 Book/CD Pack $16.95

Modern Rock Rhythm Guitar
by Danny Gill • Private Lessons
00695682 Book/CD Pack $16.95

Modes for Guitar
by Tom Kolb • Private Lessons
00695555 Book/CD Pack $17.95

Music Reading for Guitar
by David Oakes • Essential Concepts
00695192.............................. $19.99

The Musician's Guide to Recording Acoustic Guitar
by Dallan Beck • Private Lessons
00695505 Book/CD Pack $13.99

Outside Guitar Licks
by Jean Marc Belkadi • Private Lessons
00695697 Book/CD Pack $15.99

Power Plucking
by Dale Turner • Private Lesson
00695962.............................. $19.95

Practice Trax for Guitar
by Danny Gill • Private Lessons
00695601 Book/CD Pack $17.99

Progressive Tapping Licks
by Jean Marc Belkadi • Private Lessons
00695748 Book/CD Pack $15.95

Rhythm Guitar
by Bruce Buckingham & Eric Paschal • Essential Concepts
00695188 Book $17.95
00695644 VHS Video $19.95

Rock Lead Basics
by Nick Nolan & Danny Gill • Master Class
00695144 Book/CD Pack $17.99
00695910 DVD...................... $19.95

Rock Lead Performance
by Nick Nolan & Danny Gill • Master Class
00695278 Book/CD Pack $17.95

Rock Lead Techniques
by Nick Nolan & Danny Gill • Master Class
00695146 Book/CD Pack $15.95

Slap & Pop Technique for Guitar
00695645 Book/CD Pack $14.99

Technique Exercises for Guitar
by Jean Marc Belkadi • Private Lessons
00695913.............................. $14.95

Texas Blues Guitar
by Robert Calva • Private Lessons
00695340 Book/CD Pack $17.95

Ultimate Guitar Technique
by Bill LaFleur • Private Lessons
00695863.............................. $19.95